*Bountiful Baskets*

# Bountiful Baskets

## Creating Perfect Gifts for Any Occasion

### Sara Toliver
#### The White Fig

Sterling Publishing Co., Inc. New York
A Sterling/Chapelle Book

Chapelle, Ltd., Inc.,

P.O. Box 9252, Ogden, UT 84409

(801) 621-2777 • (801) 621-2788 Fax

e-mail: chapelle@chapelleltd.com

Web site: www.chapelleltd.com

Library of Congress Cataloging-in-Publication Data
Toliver, Sara.
  Bountiful baskets : creating perfect gifts for any occasion / Sara Toliver.
      p. cm.
  "A Sterling/Chapelle Book."
  Includes index.
  ISBN 1-4027-1480-7
  1. Handicraft. 2. Gift baskets. I. Title.

TT157.T59 2005
745.59--dc22

                                            2004025660

10 9 8 7 6 5 4 3 2 1

Published by Sterling Publishing Co., Inc.
387 Park Avenue South, New York, NY 10016
©2005 by Sara Toliver
Distributed in Canada by Sterling Publishing
c/o Canadian Manda Group, 165 Dufferin Street
Toronto, Ontario, Canada M6K 3H6
Distributed in Great Britain by Chrysalis Books Group PLC,
The Chrysalis Building, Bramley Road, London W10 6SP, England
Distributed in Australia by Capricorn Link (Australia) Pty. Ltd.
P. O. Box 704, Windsor, NSW 2756, Australia
Printed and Bound in China
All Rights Reserved

Sterling ISBN 1-4027-1480-7

Space would not permit the inclusion of every decorative item photographed for this book, nor could all of the designers be identified. Many of these items are available by contacting:

The White Fig
206 Historic 25th Street, Ogden, UT 84401
(801) 334-8283 • (888) 888-7829 Toll-free
Web site: www.thewhitefig.com

Why do we give gifts? There are as many reasons as there are givers: To celebrate, congratulate, and commemorate. To offer sympathy, support, or a smile. To say "Thanks," "Good luck," or "I'm thinking of you." Whatever the occasion, when we give from the heart, we give a part of ourselves.

## Baskets for whomever, whenever, whyever

We at The White Fig, a most unusual gift basket company based in historic Ogden, Utah, specialize in helping people give from the heart. We take pleasure in creating bountiful baskets that make gift giving an art and any occasion an event—and now we're delighted to share that pleasure with you.

## How to use this book

Start with **Basket Basics**, for essential tools and techniques—from brainstorming basket ideas to step-by-step instructions for planning, packing, and wrapping.

> "If it's made with your hands, it comes from the heart."
>
> Anonymous

Browse **Basket Gallery**, for a showcase of baskets arranged by theme, complete with how-tos and helpful hints. Whether you're sending holiday cheer or a get-well wish, congratulating a new grad or a new mom and dad, you'll find ideas for baskets you can assemble right away or use as a starting point for personalized presents.

Does your flair for baskets have the makings of a creative new career? Go to **Basket Business**, to learn about starting your own gift basket company. Written from the valuable perspective of an actual business owner, this section offers practical advice for every step, from deciding if a basket business is right for you to researching your market, stocking your storeroom, and building the business of your dreams.

So go ahead, put all your eggs in one basket—one *you* create!

# Contents

Introduction . . . . . . . 5

Basket Basics . . . . . . 8

Think outside the gift box • Planning your
basket • Cautions to consider • Building
your basket • Hands-on how-to's

Basket Gallery . . . 28

Gourmet Baskets . . . . . . . . . . . 30

Spa Baskets . . . . . . . . . . . . . . 36

Feminine Baskets . . . . . . . . . . . 40

Masculine Baskets . . . . . . . . . . 46

Baby and Child Baskets . . . . . . 52

Family Baskets . . . . . . . . . . . . . 66

All Occasion Baskets . . . . . . . . 72

Professional Baskets . . . . . . . . . 98

Get Well Baskets . . . . . . . . . . 102

Unique Baskets . . . . . . . . . . . 106

Basket Business . . . 110

Planning your business • Running your
business • First things first • Creating your
company • Money matters • Legal matters
• Your marketing plan • Setting up shop •
Perfecting your product • Stocking your
shelves • Pricing your product • Delivering
the goods • Growing your business

Author's Note . . . . . . 127

Metric Conversion . . 127

Index . . . . . . . . . 128

*A*nyone can go to the store, buy a ready-made item, and wrap it up. However, a gift basket you conceive and create yourself shows thoughtfulness that money *can't* buy—an expression of your relationship, caring, and history you share with the recipient.

## Think outside the gift box

The next time you need a present for a birthday, a bar mitzvah, or Bosses' Day—or for no reason, which may be the best reason of all—stop and think before you head to the mall. Why not take this opportunity to give a gift that's one of a kind? Planning and packing a basket that could only come from you is a fun, fulfilling, creative challenge, and it's easier than you may think. All you need is your own ingenuity, plus a few supplies readily available from craft suppliers, specialty shops, and Web sites. Turn the page for design strategies, assembly instructions, hands-on how-to's, and ideas we hope will inspire you.

# *Basket Basics*

## Planning your basket

Does your spouse love tennis, knitting, or classic movies? Is your best friend expecting a baby? Have your parents always talked about the trip they'll take to Alaska someday? Any special interest, special memory, or special need can spark an idea for a distinctive basket. We've provided some sample themes and brainstorming questions to get you started.

If you're sending a basket to a person or a group you don't know well—for example, a thank-you to the folks in your doctor's office—build a basket around a theme that's sure to please, such as fruit, sweets, or seasonal treats. Or work with the facts you do know: if your new neighbors come from out of state, pack a welcome basket with maps, an area magazine, and a gift certificate for a local restaurant.

## Cautions to consider

When you plan what to send, consider what *not* to send.

- Allergies/medical conditions: Be careful with food, toiletries, clothing, and scented items such as potpourri.

- Cultural/religious considerations: If the recipient keeps kosher, send only kosher foods (or no food); if she's vegan, don't send animal products; if he abstains from alcohol for religious or personal reasons, leave out the champagne.

- Special sensitivities: If someone is coping with delicate issues—a recent loss, addiction, a weight problem—consider how each item will be received. (Could your well-intentioned choice of cookies or a romantic novel touch a nerve?)

---

### Basket Brainstorming

- What does your friend (sibling, spouse, neighbor, coworker) do for a living?

- What does she do for fun?

- What's his favorite food or drink?

- Is she a sports fan? What sport? What team?

- Who's his favorite author?

- What's her favorite musical group?

- Does he like to travel? Where have you gone together?

- Do you share a favorite place? activity? memory?

- What luxury would she love, but never buy for herself?

- Could he use some support in a life change—a new home? new baby? new job?

## 50 Bountiful Baskets

You'll find many more basket ideas throughout this book—not to mention the brainstorms you'll come up with yourself. Here are some ideas to get you started.

Afternoon tea

Anniversary memories

Armchair travel

Aromatherapy

Art supplies

Baby bathtime

Back to school

Bread baking

Breakfast tray

Bride's bouquet basket

Calligraphy supplies

Candy apple makings

Car wash bucket

Cheese and crackers

Christmas tree trimming

Coffee break

Day at the beach

Easter basket (fig. 1)

First apartment starter kit

Fourth of July BBQ

Fruit *(fresh or dried)*

Gardener's tools and seeds

Get-well soup bowl

Hanukkah baskets

Housewarming

Knitting needs

Low-carb treats

Mardi Gras masks and beads

Margarita makings

Microbrew sampler

Movie night

Muffin making

Natural beauty supplies

New Year's favors

Party planning pack

Picnic paraphernalia

Puppet-making kit

Rainy-day activities

Road trip books and games

Scrapbooking supplies

Sewing basket

Shutterbug's camera bag

Slumber party survival kit

Spa day at home

Summer reading

Teacher's treats (fig. 2)

Tool kit

Valentine delicacies

Wedding party gifts

Wedding well-wishes

fig. 1

fig. 2

## Building your basket

### Container

Baskets come in all shapes, sizes, and materials—and baskets are just the beginning! Get creative with containers that reinforce your theme:

- Place housewarming gifts in an ice bucket, a punch bowl, or a wok.
- Plant a gardener's gifts in a flowerpot or watering can.
- Fill a diaper bag with new-baby necessities.
- Pack a lunch box of supplies for the first day of school.

### Filler

Filler has two functions—to fill empty space and to hold items in place. To minimize cost and maximize effect:

- Use an inexpensive filler, such as crumpled newspaper or floral foam, for a base layer.
- Top it with a more attractive filler or one that reflects your theme (coffee beans, popcorn kernels, glass stones).

- Avoid air packs and bubble wrap (which tend to lose air) and foam packing peanuts (which don't stabilize well).

If you use newspaper, note its contents; don't use the wedding announcement section in a basket for someone just divorced and don't use the obituary page at all.

### Gift items

What to put *in* that carefully chosen container? Think about items that work together to create a complete experience: not just cheese, but crackers, a knife, and a handsome serving board; not just bath products, but a fluffy towel and a scented eye mask. Points to keep in mind:

- Stick to one theme—it eliminates conflicts. Mixing items or ideas that don't relate will be confusing.
- Pick items to fit your basket's size and proportions.
- If you want to give an item too large or intangible to pack (a night of baby-sitting perhaps), use a gift certificate in its place.

### Wrapping

Let the finishing touch make a strong first impression:

- Classic cellophane shows off what's inside; to preserve a bit of mystery and add subtle color, we used iridescent cellophane (fig. 1).

fig. 1

- Tulle and netting adds an elegant touch for holidays or weddings (fig. 2).
- Shrink wrap holds contents securely for shipping.

Make your basket unique with a wrapping that enhances your theme (fig. 3). Crown your creation with a fabulous gift tag and bow.

## Hands-on how-to's

### Choose a container

Start with the right container to give your finished gift a well-designed, well-proportioned look.

1. Choose a vessel suitable for the type and number of items you'll include (fig. 4).

2. Make sure it's strong enough to support its contents. If the basket will be shipped rather than hand-delivered, keep it manageable in size and weight.

3. Select a container to suit the occasion or theme, such as a popcorn bucket for movie snacks (fig. 5). Optional: choose one that can be reused for storage or serving.

fig. 4

fig. 5

### Helpful Hint

Choosing a theme based on a color, hobby, or types of items, eliminates confusion. A basket for a hockey fan who also enjoys embroidery shouldn't include elements of both unless you include a pattern for the logo of her favorite team.

### Helpful Hint

Use glue dots (sold on sheets) to hold items in place within your basket. This works well when an arrangement of items needs discreet reinforcement to hold an unusual position.

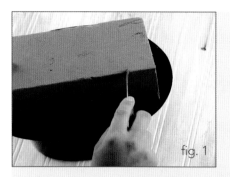
fig. 1

fig. 2

fig. 3

fig. 4

fig. 5

## Make a floral foam base

Easy-to-use floral foam at the bottom of your container makes a sturdy base for free-standing gifts that need strong support. (For lighter items, newspaper is enough.) Foam also provides a solid anchor for small gifts and filler on floral picks. (For more on these, see pages 17–18.)

1. Using container as a guide, mark foam with a sharp knife (fig. 1), then cut it to fit container opening (fig. 2). Set excess pieces aside.

2. Place foam in container and use excess to fill empty spaces (fig. 3). Make sure foam fits tightly.

## Make a fruit basket foam base

Use softer upholstery foam (available in fabric stores) to hold fresh fruit in place for a polished presentation.

1. Start with a wicker basket, newspaper, a sheet of foam slightly larger than the basket, a razor blade, fill, and 12 small pieces of fruit (fig. 4).

2. Cut six circular holes in foam, about 3" in diameter (fig. 5). Cut foam into three strips, with two holes in each strip.

3. Fill basket with crumpled newspaper (fig. 6). Place foam strips on top of newspaper, one right next to the other (fig. 7). Holes will be pushed slightly out of shape.

4. Hold a little fill under fruit and place it in one of the holes (fig. 8). Repeat until all holes are filled (fig. 9).

5. Fit smaller fruits snugly between fruits already in basket, placing fill under them as needed (fig. 10).

6. Now your basket should be full of fruit (fig. 11).

fig. 6

fig. 10

fig. 7

fig. 11

fig. 8

fig. 12

fig. 9

fig. 13

## Pack items in filler

To hold gift items in place, use a filler that will be able to support them. How much you use depends on how high you want the gifts to sit in the finished basket.

1. Place newspaper in bottom of container to create a filler base (fig. 12).

2. Top newspaper with enough filler to cover it (fig. 13).

3. Place and arrange gift items in basket (fig. 14).

4. Place remaining filler around items, propping them up and holding them in place where necessary. (In most White Fig baskets, we like to have space between items, so we make sure there's filler around every item.) See completed basket on page 16.

fig. 14

## Make a basket look full

Your basket should look like it's overflowing—without actually doing so. Make sure the basket and its contents are stable.

1. Place taller or larger items in back to create height, then fill in with remaining items (fig. 1). Don't place heavy items in front; they'll make the basket look unbalanced.

2. Adjust height of items where needed, adding more filler beneath them if necessary, to make sure each is visible (fig. 2).

3. Take a step back to see the whole basket. Adjust and rearrange where necessary.

4. Fill in space around gifts with decorative filler (fig. 3).

## Pack breakable items

When your basket must travel a long way, pack fragile items carefully and shrink wrap the basket so it won't be ruined on receipt.

1. To pack stemware, set a glass in the basket and cover the base with filler. Then use a heavier item to weigh down the fill on top of the base (fig. 4). This will keep the stemware from falling out.

2. Place plenty of fill around every breakable piece. If an item is too hard to stabilize or can't be placed in the basket safely, box and wrap it separately, then place the wrapped item in the basket.

3. Completed basket (fig. 5).

fig. 1

fig. 3

fig. 2

fig. 4

fig. 5

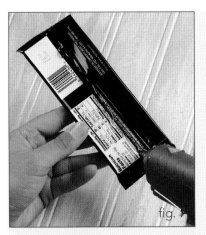

fig. 7

fig. 8

## Use decorative filler

Fancy filler adds a decorative touch and helps create a full look.

### Floral picks

Attach small gift items to floral picks (available from floral or craft suppliers) and place them randomly, anchored in floral foam. It's a great way to fill your basket and show off accent gifts.

1. On the back of the item you want to "pick," apply a line of hot glue from center to one end (fig. 7).

2. Press floral pick into glue and hold it there until glue is dry.

3. Repeat for all picks, then push picks into foam base (fig. 8).

### Ribbon sprays

Use sprays of ribbon (attached to gift items or floral picks) to give your basket color, texture, and dimension.

1. Choose several colors of curling ribbon; cut one 18" length from each. Curl each length with scissors.

2. Holding one end of each ribbon, wrap floral tape around ends to secure them together (fig. 9).

3. Apply a dab of hot glue to taped end and attach it to a gift item (fig. 10). Completed basket (fig. 11).

Optional: After Step 1, tape ends of ribbons together around a floral pick. Wrap tape about 2" down length of pick to secure.

fig. 9

fig. 10

fig. 11

fig. 1

fig. 2

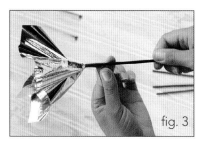

fig. 3

## *Tissue*

Tucked around the base of your basket or attached to floral picks, tissue adds fullness fast. We used metallic tissue for a glittering accent.

1. Cut tissue paper into 8" squares.

2. One square at a time, hold center and pull corners together, pinching center into a point (fig. 1).

3. Place tip of a floral pick on point of tissue paper; wrap floral tape around both tissue and pick (fig. 2).

4. Wrap tape about 2" down length of pick to secure (fig. 3). These tissues are used in the basket on page 17 (fig. 11).

## *Candy roses*

Use small gift items, such as hard-candy roses, to create unusual (and tasty!) filler.

1. Hold twisted end of a candy wrapper next to tip of a floral pick. Wrap floral tape around wrapper and pick, about 1" down length of pick (fig. 3).

2. Repeat with two more candies, placing each piece just below previous one (figs. 4 and 5). These roses are used in the basket on page 17 (fig. 11).

fig. 3

fig. 4

fig. 5

## Stack items around a basket

To give your basket a unique dimension, build a platform to stack items around the container's edges.

1. Fill bucket with newspaper and set wine inside (fig. 6).

2. Cut a rectangle of foamboard large enough to hold your items. Cut an opening in center to fit bottle's midsection (fig. 7).

3. Place cut-out board over bottle and rest it on bucket's rim. Use glue dots to secure board to rim (figs. 8 ).

4. Begin placing items on board, using glue dots to hold them in place (fig. 9).

5. Place taller items in back and shorter items in front (fig.10).

6. Fit filler around items to cover board (fig. 11).

7. Completed basket (fig. 12). If you are transporting, wrap the basket in netting or cellophane.

fig. 10

fig. 6

fig. 8

fig. 11

fig. 7

fig. 9

fig. 12

fig. 1

fig. 2

## Wrap a basket in cellophane, netting, or other wrap

Wrapping holds items in place and creates an attractive, finished look. Your choice of wrapping depends on your basket's theme and the amount of stability it needs.

1. Roll out enough cellophane or netting to completely cover basket with excess left over for gathering and tying (fig. 1).

2. Bring sides of wrapping up and over basket. Cut wrapping a few inches above basket (fig. 2).

3. Gather wrap together at top. Finish with a bow (fig 3).

## Shrink wrap

Use shrink wrap to hold items in place when transporting or shipping a basket a long distance. (If you like, you can use another, more decorative wrap on top.)

### Using a heat gun or blow-dryer

1. Roll out enough wrap to completely cover basket.

2. Bring sides of wrapping up and over basket. Gather wrapping tightly in back of basket (fig. 4).

3. Blow warm air over basket from all sides while holding wrap in place until tight (fig. 5). Be careful not to let the heat too close to the wrap—you don't want to melt a hole through it!

fig. 3

fig. 4

fig. 5

*Using a shrink-wrap machine*

1. Pull enough wrap out to fit basket.

2. Separate the two layers and place basket inside (fig. 4). Roll up excess so basket fits tightly inside wrap.

3. Press arm of machine down, sealing the wrap and separating it from the roll at the same time (fig. 5). Now the wrap is sealed on two sides.

4. On remaining sides, gather excess wrap (fig. 6) then repeat Step 3 to remove excess and seal wrap (fig. 7).

5. When the whole basket is sealed, blow warm air over basket from all sides until wrap is tight (figs. 8 and 9).

fig. 4

fig. 5

fig. 6

fig. 8

fig. 8

fig. 9

**Helpful Hint**
Camouflage puckers, wrinkles, or excess shrink wrap in a less obvious spot, like underneath or on back of the basket. This will happen less frequently with practice.

**Helpful Hint**
If you put your basket on a lazy Susan, it will be easier to turn it slowly and heat the plastic evenly.

fig. 1

### Tie a ribbon and tag the gift

Tie up the loose ends—and add a finishing touch to your basket—with a bow and tag that complement each other, the container, or the theme.

- A spa basket gets a raffia bow, with a tag made from a small manila envelope you decorate with rubber stamps (fig. 1).

- To create a riot of color, take 12 pieces of curly ribbon about 34" long, lay them flat, and staple them together in the center of a small cardboard square. Curl each strand individually, then tie them to the basket with string (fig. 2).

- Slip a small nosegay of paper flowers into the ribbon to echo the theme of a basket built around roses (fig. 3).

- To make an elegant tie, cut a piece of ¼"-wide ribbon (about 12" long or longer), then thread beads onto each end and knot the ends (fig. 4).

fig. 2

fig. 3

fig. 4

- To make an opulent wrap, cut a circle of organdy about 26" in diameter. (To bind the edge, make a rolled hem on a serger.) Place your item in the center of the fabric, pull fabric up and around, and tie with ribbon or tasseled cord (fig. 5).

- Go for the glitter with a bow made from metallic shred, which comes in long strands you can easily bunch up for tying (fig. 6).

- A fun alternative to a traditional gift tag is to write the recipient's name on a piece of paper sized to fit a small frame (fig. 7).

- To make an evocative tag, layer three pieces of paper—a solid background, a page of type, and a copy of a vintage photograph—each slightly smaller than the one below it. Glue the papers together and slip a wire hanger through a hole in the top (fig. 8).

fig. 8

fig. 5

fig. 6

fig. 7

fig. 1

- For a tag that's a gift in itself, fill a small sachet bag with aroma beads or potpourri. Slip in a paper with the name so it shows through the sheer bag (fig. 1).

- We often use our business card as a tag, with room for a message on the blank back (fig. 2).

- A Father's Day greeting card could go into an envelope inside the basket—but attached to the container by a length of twine, it gives the gift a more masculine feel (fig. 3).

- The perfect finishing touch to a Bon Voyage basket is a handsome luggage tag complete with all the pertinent information (fig.4).

fig. 2

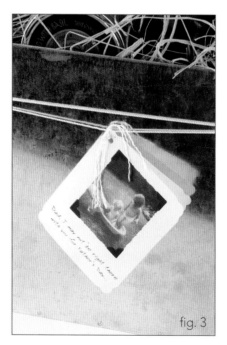

fig. 3

fig. 4

- Make a wedding-gift tag from a festive confetti bag: here, a glassine envelope filled with slips on which we've printed words such as "happiness," "forever," and "love" (fig. 5).

- We've packed this gift in a sewing box and tied it with vintage ribbon; a simple manila envelope with giver's and recipient's names completes the presentation (fig. 6).

- Create a lavish look with wire-edged ribbon, which holds its shape beautifully to give this traditional florist's bow staying power (fig. 7). For step-by-step tying instructions, see pages 26–27.

- A basket of culinary delights includes a recipie holder which holds the name of the lucky recipient (fig.8). Any photo holder with coils will work.

fig. 8

fig. 5

fig. 6

fig. 7

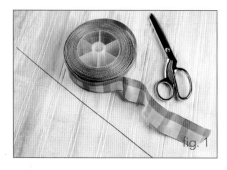

fig. 1

fig. 2

fig. 3

fig. 4

*Florist's bow*

1. Start with 18" length of floral wire, scissors, and wire-edged ribbon (fig. 1).

2. Holding ribbon between thumb and middle finger of your left hand, pull ribbon out to desired length (fig. 2).

3. Give ribbon one half twist; hold center of twist (fig. 3).

4. Make a loop and hold it between thumb and middle finger (fig. 4).

5. Repeat Steps 2 and 3, alternating sides, making each loop slightly larger (figs. 5 and 6).

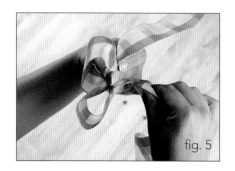

fig. 5

fig. 6

6. When you've created the middle loop and three on each side, cut ribbon, leaving a 6" tail (figs. 7 and 8).

7. Take a new piece of ribbon, leave a 6" end free (on the opposite side from the tail in Step 6), and make two loops on each side (fig. 9). Cut ribbon, leaving a 6" tail (fig. 10).

8. Thread floral wire under thumb and between fingers, then wrap around center of bow (figs. 11 and 12).

9. With your right hand, twist wire ends together (fig. 13)

10. Pull loops out to sides, working from top to bottom and alternating sides (fig. 14).

11. Position loops as desired (fig. 15).

12. Cut each ribbon end into a V shape (figs. 16 and 17).

13. Attach bow to your basket with excess wire.

fig. 7

fig. 8

fig. 12

fig. 16

fig. 9

fig. 13

fig. 17

fig. 10

fig. 14

## Basket Worksheet

Fill in the elements of your basket as you decide on them. Check them off as you complete them.

Theme _____

Container _____

Filler _____

Gift items _____

Wrap _____

Bow _____

Tag _____

fig. 11

fig. 15

# Basket Gallery

When customers come to us at The White Fig, we listen closely to what they need—whether it's a corporate gift or a deeply personal message to a dear friend—and we work *closely* with them to find the best way to realize their vision. Over the years, we've developed the craft of creating just the right gift, in the right style, at the right price—and we want you to know that you can do the same.

## A gallery of gifts

In the chapters that follow, you'll find dos, don'ts, and detailed advice for designing baskets of all kinds (plus helpful hints, basket ideas, and tips for staying within your budget). But mostly you'll find *baskets*—more than 100 of them—that we've created for our customers. As you peruse these photographs and practical guidelines, we hope you'll have fun planning and packing birthday baskets, baby bundles, and portable spas—and we trust you'll be inspired with ideas for bountiful baskets of your own!

# Gourmet Baskets

The gift of food, deliciously decadent or simply sustaining, is always welcome. You can design a gourmet basket that's perfect for almost any purpose—a housewarming or a holiday, a wedding or an anniversary, a thank-you to a vendor or a client—even if you don't know the tastes of the person you're sending it to. (If you do know them, you can create a really personal gift: for a wine connoisseur, for example, pack a couple of well-chosen bottles in an attractive ice bucket with a corkscrew, glasses, and a pocket guide to wine.)

## Food for thought

When you plan a gourmet basket, consider:

- **Who's receiving it?** If you're sending a basket to a group in an office, include foods that don't need cooking and that everyone can share. If you know of any food allergies or diet restrictions, plan accordingly. (You wouldn't, for example, send wine or beer to someone whose religion forbids it.)

- **What's the theme?** Be creative! Build a basket around a food or beverage (tea, fruit, nuts); a cuisine (Southwestern, Thai, Italian, Greek); or a lifestyle (low-carb or low-fat treats for the health conscious).

- **What else besides food?** Make your basket more fun (and more practical) with items that enhance the edibles: a cheese knife, a tea infuser, a cookbook, coasters, coffee mugs.

**Dollar Saver Tip**

Use inexpensive, bulky items such as crackers to make your basket look lavishly full. Then slip smaller, costlier items—gourmet cheeses, preserves, marzipan—into the space remaining.

**Basket Idea**

Spotlight a part of the country or the world with a basket of regional foods. A Pacific Northwest basket might include a sampler of salmon, fruits, berries, coffees, and jam on a serving platter; a Japanese basket could hold chopsticks, rice bowls, and a calligraphy brush with paper and ink.

**Helpful Hint**

Don't spoil your basket with spoiled food! Use shelf-stable items whenever you can. Avoid melt-prone items such as cheese and chocolate in hot weather. Any time you ship perishables in a basket, send it overnight to ensure freshness. This will reduce the risk of spoilage.

**Above:** It's surprisingly simple to create a gourmet basket of the same style and quality you'd find at a national retailer. Here, the shapes and symmetry of fresh fruit—held in place by a cut-out foam sheet over newspaper, as shown on pages 14–15 in *Basket Basics* —create a pleasing array in a classic wicker basket.

**Previous Page:** For someone who loves to cook (or wants to start), pack an Italian basket with the fixings for a gourmet meal: olive oil, sun-dried tomatoes, a specialty sauce, utensils, perhaps a cookbook. Here, it's packed in a stainless-steel colander with an equally functional filler: the pasta itself!

**Above:** Set your gift a little apart in a basket that's wire, not wicker. You won't need a foam base here if you pack the basket with filler and nest the fruit inside. Remember, when shipping food, overnight it for freshness—and watch the weather: if it's very cold or hot, there's more risk of freezing or spoilage.

**Opposite:** Who wouldn't rise and shine for this attractive, appetizing breakfast basket? Start with a straw-filled base that suggests farm-fresh goodness, then slip in muffin makings and mini tins, little jams and marmalades, pancake mix and maple syrup—whatever you think will brighten the morning most.

# *Gourmet Baskets*

# *Gourmet Baskets* continued

**Above:** For a "cosmopolitan" girl, fill an ice bucket with the makings of a perfect Cosmo—mix, glasses, sugar—plus color-coordinated goodies to go with it. (They needn't all be liquid, or even edible.) Customize this idea for any favorite drink, from margaritas to martinis (include a classic shaker).

**Opposite:** Give fresh fruit a finishing touch by packing it in a pretty fruit bowl they'll use long after the fruit is eaten. Because it needs no packing material, this basket is easy to assemble, and it's also easy to ship: just shrink-wrap it securely and box it with foampopcorn or other cushioning.

# Spa Gift Baskets

We all need a little pampering sometimes—but thos who need it most are the ones who don't have *time* to take time for themselves. That's where you come in.

You can soothe the stressed-out souls in your life with gift baskets that put the pleasure and peace of a spa within easy reach. To create wonderfully personal presents, choose from a wide range of bath, shower, and spa products: bubble bath, bath salts, shower gel, loofahs, pumice stones, manicure and pedicure kits, eye masks. (For a truly luxurious gift, include a plush towel, a bathrobe, or a gift certificate for a professional massage.)

## Rules for relaxation

Things to keep in mind when you plan a spa basket:

- **They're not just for women.** Stress-relieving supplies are just as suitable for a man—or for anyone who needs to unwind: an overworked executive, an administrative assistant, a new father, a college student facing exams.

- **They're great for couples.** Customize a basket-for-two with things that make relaxing romantic: candles, massage oil, whatever the imagination suggests.

- **They work on holidays.** Give a spa basket for Mother's Day or Father's Day, on Valentine's Day or Christmas, to say thank you or congratulations or simply when you feel it's needed.

## $ Dollar Saver Tip

In place of pricey designer products, choose pleasingly packaged and scented items from more reasonable retailers. Your local drugstore may stock soaps, salts, lotions, and loofahs that supply a satisfying spa experience without blowing the budget.

## B Basket Idea

For a soul-soothing experience, build an aromatherapy basket around essential oils and potpourri in your scent of choice (rose relieves melancholy, sandalwood is calming and grounding). Then add candles and a CD of nature sounds, soft classical music, or meditative chant.

## ! Helpful Hint

Don't combine food and bath items in the same basket. We know that delicious foods can be a pleasant part of a pampering experience—but food items packaged with scented bath products may absorb their aroma. (And eating sweets that taste like soap isn't very relaxing.)

**Above:** A spa basket should stimulate the senses, not overwhelm them. For a truly relaxing retreat, balance variety with consistency in look and style (as in this flowerpot basket anchored by coordinating products); avoid aroma conflict by selecting liquids, lotions, and salts with the same scent.

**Previous Page:** Soothe her stress (or his) with a basket that supplies spa essentials from head to toe. This all-in-one presentation includes bath soaps, lotions and oils, sponge and loofah, plus foot-massaging gel slippers to wear to and from the tub and sparkling water to replenish from within.

**Above:** Spa gets a stylish spin here with a streamlined selection of bath products—all from the same line, with bold graphic labels. For extra punch, it's all packed in a softly colored bucket with a perfectly practical filler: bath salts ready to scoop right into a waiting tub.

**Opposite:** Broaden your spa basket's appeal beyond the bath! This imaginative basket of spa supplies scented with soothing lavender, packed in a handsome watering-can container and crowned with a living plant, evokes a connection to nature and the calm of the countryside.

# Feminine Baskets

Is your mom a movie buff? Does your girlfriend love her garden? Use what you know about the women in your life to design baskets customized for their interests. Perfect for any occasion—to celebrate a birthday or Christmas, to help a retiree enjoy her newfound free time—these gifts are so personal they're sure to please.

## Making special interests special

- **Keep it together.** Brainstorm one theme and stick to it. Your sister may love tennis and travel, but combining both in a single basket will only create confusion.

- **Be a creative collector.** You might supply a knitter with all the tools for a single project, encourage a beginning artist with a basket of basic needs, or give a golfer all the essentials of a great day on the links: golf balls and tees in fun colors, club covers, a golf glove, sunscreen, lip balm, even a first aid kit.

- **Pack it perfectly.** Choose a container that will keep giving pleasure long after it's unpacked. Stash sewing supplies in a classic sewing basket; stow supplies for the travel buff in a convenient carry-on; for a party-giver, stack coasters, cookbook, and a CD of cocktail-hour tunes on a stylish serving tray.

### $ Dollar Saver Tip
If you can't spend much on a brand-new container, thrift shops and tag sales may yield treasures you'll have fun rejuvenating. Polish an old punch bowl, scrape and stencil a simple wooden box, or paint a pretty pattern on a flower-pot—the effort will make your gift even more special.

### B Basket Idea
Create a bookworm's basket in a tote, filled with titles from a favorite author. The titles may suggest suitable snacks to include (such as, *Like Water for Chocolate*). Add bookmarks, a clip-on book light, or even a biography of the author to round out the basket.

### ! Helpful Hint
If she's already well supplied with the tools of her hobby, don't give up—just give her something she wouldn't buy herself: for a knitter, skeins of luxurious cashmere; for a reader, a first edition of a favorite book; for a musician, concert tickets or enrollment in a master class.

**Above:** How does her garden grow? With thoughtfully chosen tools, inspiring ideas, and a little help from you. Here, an easy-to-clean wire basket carries all the makings of beautiful blooms: garden supplies (trowel, shears, gloves), flowerpots in cool celadon and cream, and a bag of bulbs ready to plant.

**Previous Page:** We believe you can never have too much chocolate—and if you know someone who agrees, pack her a basket of sweet treats she wouldn't buy for herself. Here, luscious liqueur and candies of all kinds—plain, fancy, flavored—are packed in an elegant carrier that's the rich hue of milk chocolate itself.

**Opposite:** Who's to say a basket has to be practical? Sometimes it's enough just to surround ourselves with things we enjoy. So if she loves roses, give her a basket full of them, figuratively speaking: potpourri, toiletries, a rose-printed picture frame, and silk or fresh flowers as a finishing touch.

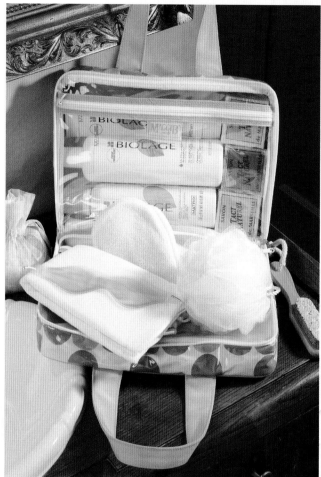

**Above:** A rose is a rose is a . . . beautiful basket *brimming* with roses! This large, shallow basket with high curved handle allows plenty of room for floral fancies—from art and a handsomely bound blank book to candle holders and rose-colored tapers—with artificial blooms as an overflowing border.

**Above:** Form and function meet fun and fashion in this lively-patterned makeup bag. Packed with beauty essentials—from soaps and lotions to a gel mask for soothing tired eyes—it's a perfect companion for traveling, grooming at the gym, or freshening up at the office before heading out on the town.

**Above:** Keep her in stitches with this imaginatively packaged kit of seamstress's supplies. When she needs to replace a button, she can dip into two jars full; for mending, altering, or making new creations, she'll find needles to suit any fabric and thread in all the colors of the rainbow.

**Above:** Sometimes a container suggests its own contents—like this gorgeous ceramic iced-tea urn complete with tap and lid. Filled with tea bags (choose her favorite brand, blend, or herbal variety) and sugar sticks to stir in flavor, it's a source of constant refreshment for a serious sipper.

# Masculine Baskets

What can you give the man who has everything? The gift of your time and thoughtfulness. Consider the things you know he enjoys—is he an antique-car aficionado? a talented chef?—then choose one theme (more than one gets confusing) as the basis for a gift basket custom-designed to suit his interests.

## A man, a plan, a basket

Is he a . . .

- **Sports fan?** Help him root for his team in style! Pack a duffel bag with a t-shirt, a cap, and other branded memorabilia. For a really special occasion, throw in tickets to a game or race.

- **Hunter or fisherman?** Outfit him for a day outdoors with sunscreen, lip balm, hand warmers, and a cooler of snacks and drinks—plus a frame to hold the photo that will commemorate his prize. ("It was *this big . . .*")

- **Builder, fixer, or gardener?** If he can spend hours tinkering under the hood, digging in the dirt, or patiently stripping off layers of paint in hopes that there's beautiful woodwork beneath, gather the supplies he needs in a sturdy bucket or toolbox.

- **Lover of the finer things?** For the cigar connoisseur, fill a humidor with a choice of fine cigars, plus a cutter, a lighter, an ashtray—and air freshener!

## $ Dollar Saver Tip

If cost is a concern, don't buy elaborate items; let your basket's value come from the thoughtful way you choose and combine them. A gift for the computer whiz could include a personalized mouse pad, a screen cloth, a can of compressed air to dust his keyboard, and the latest issue of a computer magazine.

## B Basket Idea

For a shutterbug, fill a camera bag with film, a tripod, a lens cloth, and filters to create special effects. Add a photo album, a frame, and a book on technique or his favorite photographer. If he has digital capability, tuck in a memory card compatible with his camera, plus computer software to retouch his photos.

## ! Helpful Hint

Do you know a man who's notoriously hard to buy for? Any of these baskets would work well as a gift for Christmas, Father's Day, an anniversary, or Valentine's minus the frills.

**Above:** Handyman special! This workhorse of a tool box, filled with implements of every size and description, ensures he'll never have to stop work in the middle of a project because he can't find his #3 Phillips screwdriver. Include items he might not buy for himself, like a sleek, bright mini-flashlight. Use penny nails or screws as filler.

**Previous Page:** Ah, the thrill of the grill! Give your master chef everything he needs to create a barbe-cued feast: utensils, skewers, sauces, seasonings, a wire brush for cleaning, and a fun apron to keep *him* clean. This is one gift that pays dividends— you may get to sample the results!

**Opposite:** Does he take better care of his car than he does of himself? Help him buff his ride to a beau-tiful shine with cleansers, cloths, and polishes packed in a sturdy plastic bucket. To make wash day even more fun, add a CD of his favorite music to pop into the stereo while he brushes the upholstery.

**Above:** To pack a basket for the duffer in your life, start with a wire bucket (the kind you'd find at the driving range), then add supplies both practical and whimsical: practice balls, ball markers, tees, a book of golf tips or stories, even a coupon for refreshments at the 19th hole.

**Above:** This classic fishing basket, filled with supplies for a day on the water, is easy to customize for a fly fisherman or reel fisherman—and even for a specific stretch of water or time of year. Just ask the pros at the shop what they're biting on. (The fish, that is.)

# Masculine Baskets

**Above:** Even if you don't know his most personal interests, you can still create a thoughtful basket that's sure to be welcome. Any man will appreciate this morning survival kit, with daily paper, coffee, mugs, and a luxuriously soft robe, making it pleasurable (or at least *possible*) to rise and shine.

**Above:** Forget about foampeanuts—real ones taste much better. For the brew lover in your life, pack some longnecks in a galvanized bucket with peanuts (in the shell) as edible filler. Add his favorite snacks, and unless you're positive the bottles have twist-off caps, don't forget the opener!

# Baby and Child Baskets

*G*ift baskets aren't just for grown-ups! They're also a delightful way to broaden children's horizons, make birthdays and holidays special, or welcome a new baby into the world. And—whether you're packing a beautiful basket for expectant parents to open at a shower, supplying practical necessities for the first few days at home, or combining a portable lap desk with coloring books, paper, and nontoxic crayons to spark an older child's creativity—they're great fun to make, because the occasions are so joyful.

## Handle with care

Making baskets for children (or homes with children) calls for special considerations:

- **Stay safe.** In a baby basket, be sure all bath products are very gentle and all sleepwear is flame-retardant. Leave out anything a child's parents do not want him or her to play with or eat. And be aware of other children in the home—toys perfect for a four-year-old may be a risk to her infant brother.

- **Keep it kid-friendly.** Make your gifts age-appropriate (small parts pose a choking hazard for little ones); visually appealing (try drawing on wrapped candies to make ladybugs and bumblebees); and full of interactive elements to keep children entertained.

- **Make it memorable.** If the occasion is a birth or a first birthday, include something the parents can keep as a memento—perhaps an engraved keepsake, a memory book, or a durable card.

### Dollar Saver Tip
Instead of expensive baby clothes or toys, give something you've made yourself—or something you will do yourself, such as a coupon for babysitting. New parents may need this kind of help even more than costly gifts!

### Basket Idea
Ignite a child's imagination with a puppet-making basket that includes all the essentials—tube socks, pompoms, google eyes, nontoxic craft glue, felt, pipe cleaners—plus a book with instructions for making different kinds of puppets.

### Helpful Hint
In a baby basket, hide a little something that's just for the new mom—she needs special treatment too!—and include a small gift for any other children in the family to soothe possible pangs of jealousy.

**Above:** Dinner at eight! A translucent plastic container inspired by Chinese takeout boxes (a welcome sight in any busy, hungry household) overflows with pastel grass filler and a colorful array of gifts for baby.

**Previous Page:** Ducks ahoy! Wherever a new baby's bathing, this little boat sails in with ducks of several varieties (rubber, stuffed, soap), plus an adorable shirt and blanket that continue the nautical theme. It's a great way to help baby take to bathtime like—well, like a duck to water.

**Above:** Opened up, the takeout box turns out to be a pretty, whimsical wrapping for baby's own "place setting": a bib, cup, and keepsake silver spoon. To continue the dinner theme, include a gift certificate the new parents can use for a real takeout meal—one from a restaurant or one you cook and deliver.

**Opposite:** Compartmentalized in a cheerfully painted wooden box, this broad selection of baby supplies (from food to shampoo to rubber duck) looks much more appealing than it would if it were jumbled together—and once emptied, the nine-compartment container can be used to organize clothes, toiletries, or toys.

*Take a picture
Of baby and me.
Once a week,
Same day you know.
Just 24 poses
and you will see
how precious we are
and how much we grow.*

**Above:** Memories in the making! Baby's first teddy bear comes with a camera full of film and framed instructions, inviting parents to create an ever-changing record of the new arrival's first weeks. *Take a picture Of baby and me. Once a week, Same day you know. Just 24 poses and you will see how precious we are and how much we grow.*

**Opposite:** Once upon a time there was a gift basket that was made from a beautiful book rack, and filled with thoughtful treasures including a floppy-eared patchwork bunny, baby blocks, and other baby necessities.

Once upon a time...

**Above:** Even the most practical gift basket can be attractive and appealing. Everything in this batch of baby supplies has a down-to-earth use—from the container, a tub designed for infant bathing, to the cotton-ball filler that creates a bubble-bath look—but the presentation makes it a pleasure to open.

**Opposite:** It's a sleepover! Give a child and his or her guests all the makings of slumber-party fun: an age-appropriate movie and snacks, supplies for easy crafts projects (such as plastic beads for stringing necklaces), fixings for decorating (and eating) cupcakes, flashlights tucked in the back for after lights-out.

**Above:** These sweet-treat baskets are abuzz with kid appeal! Attach decorated cookies to floral picks, anchor them in a base of floral foam, then fill containers with wrapped candies. Use foil-wrapped chocolate ladybugs and bumblebees (also on floral picks) for a delicious finishing touch.

**Helpful Hint**

Increase the value of your gift by choosing a container that can be reused after the goodies inside are gone.

**Above:** An older child will appreciate this exuberant basket packed with the makings of a birthday bash. Tuck in candies, candles, party favors, a festive bottle of birthday punch, and a camera to record the fun. Add a fun frame to hold the favorite shot of the day and a wrapped gift to prolong the suspense. Line the box's rim with store-bought sprays of "curly ribbon" to create the overflowing effect.

**Above:** Color their world—or let them color it themselves! Pack pencils, washable markers, and nontoxic crayons with coloring books and sketchpads in a sturdy container that can be used to store art supplies long after the gift is opened. Who knows? You might inspire a miniature Michelangelo in the making.

**Above:** You can make special-interest gift baskets for children as well as adults (except the interests are more likely to involve playing in sand). Here, a durable, colorful dump truck carries a payload of distinctive toys—almost as much fun to play with as they are to dump, reload, and dump again.

**Above:** Keep a boisterous group entertained the healthy way with mini soccer balls and softballs (or any age-appropriate sports equipment) for hours of active play, plus suitable snacks for when their energy flags. (If you prefer, substitute juice for the sports drinks and other foods for the granola bars.)

**Opposite:** Want to be sure your container will be used long after the "basket" is emptied? Choose a classic like this red wagon, then load it up with all sorts of colorful plastic playthings to keep kids happily occupied: jump ropes, bubble blowers, sandbox supplies, and, of course, a bouncy ball.

**Above:** For a different take on a child's beach basket, choose a vintage (or vintage-look) pail that evokes a seaside idyll, then add just a few carefully chosen accoutrements: sunglasses and shovel in coordinating colors, seashells for a fun "filler," plus sunscreen to keep a water baby sun-safe.

**Opposite:** What's more fun than a day at the pool? A day at the pool with cool pool toys. Start with a water-worthy bucket (a must to corral poolside necessities), then add tools, toys, and towels at will. Add child-friendly sunscreen, if you like, to make it a *safe* day in the sun.

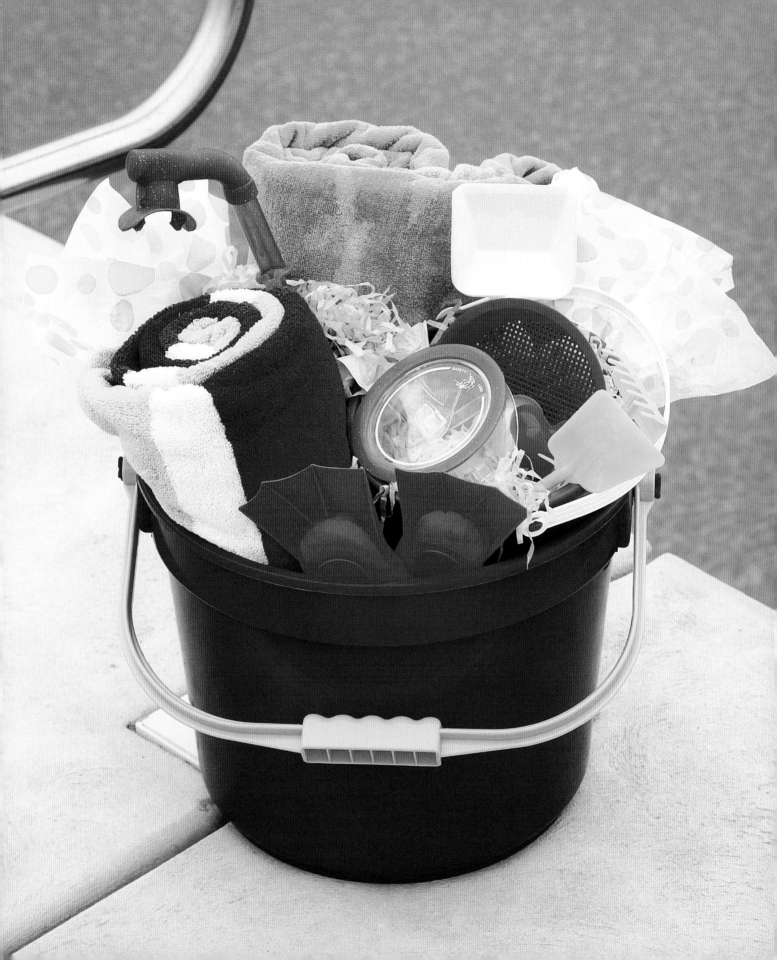

# Family Baskets

*F*un for the whole family! It sounds simple—but it's not so simple when the "whole family" includes two adults, a ten-year-old, a five-year-old, and a dog. Still, with a little creativity and the ideas we offer here to get you started, you really *can* create a family gift basket that will please everybody. (Even the dog.)

## Questions to ask

- **What's the occasion?** If you're giving a family basket at the holidays, include treats and decorations; if it's a housewarming gift, find something small to decorate each family member's new space; if it's a welcome-to-the-neighborhood, include facts on local family activities and, if you like, an invitation to a children's play date.

- **What does the family do together?** If they're hikers, boaters, or musicians, you can build a basket around the activities they enjoy. If they have a connection to another part of the country or the world, you might highlight that culture through foods, books, and toys.

- **What are the children's ages and interests?** If you know, choose a little something to please everyone individually. If you don't know, build a basket around a theme you can be sure everyone will enjoy, such as all the fixings for homemade pizza or a cozy movie night.

### $ Dollar Saver Tip
To fill out a snack or movie basket without going over budget, include an inexpensive board or card game for another activity everyone can enjoy. Add to their fun (but not to your bill) by slipping in a treat for the family pet.

### B Basket Idea
Pack a "trip basket" for a family on the go. Fill a large duffel bag with a first-aid kit, moist wipes, car-friendly snacks and drinks, CDs, crossword puzzles, word-search games, journals for older children to take trip notes, and disposable cameras for each child to document the journey.

### ! Helpful Hint
Let a favorite family film suggest a container and its contents. To make a *Finding Nemo* basket, you might choose a clear plastic tote printed with colorful fish, then add a Go Fish card deck, a book on undersea life, and goldfish crackers. Don't forget a videotape or DVD of the movie!

**Above:** Lights . . . camera . . . popcorn! Set the scene for family movie night with classic cinema snacks and drinks, packed in a popcorn bucket with fluffy popped kernels as decorative filler. (It's not for eating; the microwave popcorn pack takes care of that.) Don't forget to include a film all ages can enjoy!

**Previous Page:** Pizza, a perennial favorite, is that much more delicious when the whole family prepares it together. Get them started with a gift basket that gathers all the fixings—sauce, spices, utensils—atop a pizza stone or deep-dish pan. (If your basket will be hand-delivered, you can even include the cheese!)

**Above:** This refreshingly bright enamel bucket is really a drink dispenser (note the tap at the bottom)—but it easily does double duty as a dispenser of solid-state snacks. (Not coincidentally, any or all of them would go very well with a favorite cold drink.)

**Opposite:** When winter's at its worst, or when circumstances keep a family cooped up, a hot cocoa basket helps them enjoy a cozy evening *in*. Here, enameled mugs (make sure there's one for each family member) echo the container's texture and trim; marshmallows, snacks, and cocoa mix add finishing touches.

**Above:** Get the scoop on family fun with a basket full of fixings to help them put on their sundae best! Pack pretty dishes or parfait glasses with all the toppings you can find or fit—fudge, butterscotch, sprinkles, cherries—plus a scoop for serving. (In other words, everything but the ice cream.)

**Opposite:** For all the fun of a towering ice cream cone with none of the mess, we packed this old-fashioned painted bucket with snacks that don't melt: color-coordinated soft drinks, popcorn, and candy sticks.

What better way to celebrate a birthday, graduation, engagement, or holiday than with a bountiful gift basket that makes the special occasion that much more special? Instead of focusing on hobbies or interests, let the meaning of the milestone (plus what you know of the recipient's taste) suggest the contents of your basket, from scrumptious foods to sentimental keepsakes to supplies for a new phase of life.

## A basket for all reasons

With a little thought, you can create a gift that's suitable to wish a loved one good luck, express your thanks to a friend, even extend your condolences to someone who's been bereaved. Some points to guide your planning:

- **For a wedding,** what's the couple's age range? Have they been married before? Are they setting up housekeeping in a new home?

- **For an anniversary,** what are their ages? Is it the first anniversary or the twenty-first? You might give a nod to tradition by including customary anniversary gifts (paper, china, silver) or give the tradition your own creative spin.

- **For a housewarming,** is she moving into a place that needs a lot of TLC? Is he living on his own for the first time?

### $ Dollar Saver Tip
Maybe you can't afford a basket full of real gold but you can still mark a beloved couple's fiftieth anniversary with traditional flair! Include a photo in a gold-tone frame, sprinkle your basket with gold-wrapped chocolate coins, or tie it all up with gold-colored netting and ribbon.

### Basket Idea
Welcome a new college grad to the working world with a basket of business essentials: a planner, a desk calendar, a business-card holder, a stress ball to squeeze when the going gets tough. Add a tie for him, a scarf or professional-looking clutch for her.

### ! Helpful Hint
To make a holiday basket personal, connect the symbols of the season with something specific in the recipient's life. For example, help a wine lover celebrate the Fourth of July with a selection of American reds and whites in a blue picnic hamper.

**Above:** Stacking boxes in different pastel colors, shapes, and sizes coordinate to create a tantalizing impression: what could be inside? Tie them together with a pretty ribbon to create a tower that looks good enough to eat.

**Previous Page:** When filled with chocolate instead of chop suey, takeout boxes are transformed into a thoughtful, tasty thank-you. Fill each box with a different kind of sweet, covering all flavor bases—fruity, nutty, savory. (Chopsticks optional.)

**Above:** Once unpacked, the pastel stacked tins open up to reveal sweet treats suited to each box's shape: rows of cupcakes in the square box, a cake perfectly sized for the round one, cookies piled high in the tall one. Easy to make with home-baked or store-bought goods, this is a great way to show your appreciation.

**Opposite:** Toast a friend who deserves your thanks with a frosty margarita on the rocks . . . literally! This bright, fun basket includes drink mix, glasses, and salt for the rims, with rocks as filler. (The rocks will make the basket very heavy; to make a version you can ship, replace the rocks with coarse salt.)

**Above:** When a loved one suffers a loss, we're sometimes at a loss to offer comfort. But you can show your support with a basket of thoughtfully chosen items to fill practical needs (here, notepaper for the thank-you's they'll be writing), along with a book of poems or prayers to help the heart heal. The container is a box to hold mementos—the obituary, program, letters, and any other items that may be important at a difficult time.

**Above:** In Eastern traditions, the bamboo is a powerful symbol of good luck—and it also makes an elegant gift for sending luck to someone in your life. Here, bamboo gets an extra good-fortune boost from a four-leaf clover encased in Lucite (perfect for desk or dorm room) and a scattering of clover coins.

**Opposite:** For a new grad heading out on his or her own, help soften the shock of the real world (no more dining hall!) with a basket of necessities for a new home: easy-to-cook foods and mixes, cleaning and housekeeping basics, all packed in a sturdy basket that's ready to be refilled with laundry.

**Above:** Take the metaphor of "housewarming" a step further with a basket you deliver on site! When the new occupant is out, you slip in and stuff the oven with a generous selection of groceries. This idea works well with a fridge or microwave, too, and it's a great way to help out a new grad or newlyweds.

**Opposite:** Moving into a new home is tiring! Help them start those first few mornings right with a highly caffeinated gift basket. Include whatever you think they could use: ground or whole-bean coffee, a thermal carafe in an eye-opening color, perhaps rock-sugar stirring sticks. Add real beans as filler.

**Above:** Doing the dishes becomes an unprecedented pleasure with this ingeniously packaged housewarming kit, in which six separate cups hold all the necessities: sponges, brushes, scented dishwashing liquid, cloths, and linen towels. Don't forget hand lotion in a complementary scent to soothe chapped hands.

**Above:** To help them make a new house feel like home, send supplies for painting: a choice of rollers and brushes, a stirrer, and tape for marking edges, switch plates, or window frames. Pack it all in a shiny paint can—and, if you can manage it, wrap the finished basket in a drop cloth for delivery.

**Opposite:** Fill a well-made wicker basket with laundry needs—detergent, fabric softener, clothespins, hangers—to help new homeowners settle in. (This way, they won't have to unpack twenty boxes to find their laundry supplies!)

**Above:** If your friend loves to garden (or if the new place will provide her first plot of her own), pack a basket that takes housewarming back to its roots. Here, a sturdy pail holds things to wear, wield, and plant: gardener's gloves and clogs, a flower-patterned apron, tools, stakes, and seeds.

**Opposite:** This lavish assortment of cleaning and laundry products, stowed in a stamped-metal carrier, makes a luxurious housewarming gift for someone who's house-proud. Packed in jars and stoppered bottles in a fresh spring palette, even the *products* are beautiful—just think how the house will look!

**Above:** If the new couple is moving into a new home (and especially if they're living on their own for the first time), help them stock their kitchen with a shopping cart full of staples, including the makings of a few simple meals. (You'll save them a trip to the store on the way home from the honeymoon.)

**Above:** Designing a gift basket for an occasion such as a wedding is a joy in itself. This elegant presentation sticks to traditional tones and themes, with creamy silk roses as filler, a pair of champagne flutes for the couple to toast their future, and an album to fill with pictures of their special day.

**Above:** Pack an elegant serving bowl for the mother of the bride to help her keep her strength up. Include deliciously rich chocolate or another indulgence you know she'll enjoy along with bowls for serving, a knife for sharing and a decorative frame to hold a sentimental photo of the occasion.

**Above:** Pack a romantic picnic for two! This hamper holds plates and utensils in convenient straps, so once the newlyweds have consumed *your* picnic, they can use the basket again and again. (A basket like this may not require any extra filler, because the items fit so snugly in the structured container.)

**Above:** For an imaginative way to mark a couple's milestone, create a massage basket for two. Here, we've packed the essentials of a soothing rubdown (from oils and towels to a candle and potpourri for atmosphere) in a wicker case that echoes the theme of natural balance and wellness.

**Above:** Help them celebrate in classic style with an anniversary basket of wine or champagne. Pack a silver wine cooler with stemware, plus bottle opener and stopper. For a truly personal gift, have the cooler engraved with their monogram or wedding date.

**Opposite:** Did they have their first date at a French restaurant (or, for that matter, in France)? Use a couple's personal history to design a really personal anniversary gift, such as this tempting array of French wine, cheese, and bakery-fresh bread in a market basket lined with linen.

**Above:** Open your heart to your Valentine with a basket that's already done the opening for you (in a plastic container with heart-shaped cutouts to let high-contrast filler show through). Include silk flowers, conversation hearts, a book or poem, a picture of you together—whatever says "love" to you.

**Opposite:** This tower of treats broadcasts your message loud and clear! Perfect to give your partner on your anniversary or for Valentine's, the stacking boxes can be filled with delectable edibles, mementos, or other treats you can enjoy together. Once they're stacked, tie the boxes together with wide ribbon or netting.

I LOVE YOU! I LOVE
YOU! I LOVE
I LOVE YOU! I LOVE
YOU! I LOVE
YOU! I LOVE YOU! I LOVE
I LOVE

**Above:** Time for spring cleaning! An Easter basket for a special lady, we've packed this basket with bathtime treats: soaps, lotions, and salts inspired by the cool pastels and fresh scents of the season. Fill the hollow plastic eggs with whatever strikes your fancy—bath beads, wrapped candies—and tuck them into the empty spaces.

**Opposite:** This imaginative take on the timeless Easter basket is actually a little square of lawn dotted with faux eggs ready for the hunt (with a dapper rabbit standing watch). This basket is meant to be a decoration so whether you use artificial grass or the real thing in a planter, it's a great way to capture the essence of spring.

**Above:** Three cheers for the red, white, and blue! Supply your friends for Fourth-of-July fun with a selection of soft drinks, snacks, and color-coordinated decorations in a galvanized pail decoupaged with Old Glory's stars and stripes. Why, it's practically your patriotic duty.

**Opposite:** It seems that Santa left his boot behind (a tight fit in the chimney, perhaps?), so why not take the opportunity to fill it with all the treats of the season? Paint a papier-mâché boot and frost it with glitter. Include candy canes, trimmings for tree or window, and homemade goodies secured in red and green plastic wrap.

**Above:** Set the scene for Christmas cheer with this delightful scene of Old World carolers and musicians making their rounds. (Or use any other figures you prefer—reindeer, angels, snowmen) This basket is designed to be a decorative centerpiece, but once the collectible papier-mâché figurines are removed, the cake stand and cloche are perfect for serving holiday sweets.

**Above:** Brightly colored stacking boxes (these stack up to a classic Nutcracker soldier) make perfect holders for Christmas goodies of different sizes. Try filling one with a small personal gift, another with a special ornament for the tree, a third with cookies or candies you've made yourself.

**Opposite:** Charlie Brown would be proud to trim this little tree—but your friends may want to use the shiny ornaments in this festive basket to deck a somewhat grander evergreen. Perfect to bring to a holiday party, give to a group of coworkers, or supply for a young couple's first Christmas in their own home.

**Above:** This New Year's bonbon basket evokes auld lang syne with a warmer palette of colors— gold, red, bright pink and blue—in a container that's filled to brimming (and transparent to let all the gold show through). Exuberant sprays of decorative filler make these simple contents shine.

**Opposite:** For a fun way to ring in the New Year, cut a foam base for a container shaped like an upturned top hat. Then use floral picks to create a forest of festive treats—noisemakers, chocolate bars, candy champagne bottles. Even the tissue filler is attached to floral picks! (See page 17 in *Basket Basics* for techniques.)

# Professional Baskets

All too often, we define ourselves (and others) by the question "What do you do?" So why not make that fixation the foundation of a fun, thoughtful gift? A basket based on the livelihood of a loved one (or a client or colleague) makes a great thank-you, holiday greeting, or Bosses' Day gift—and depending on your relationship to the recipient, it can be as lighthearted or as genuinely practical as you like.

## Work your basket!

- **Is it a joke gift?** Then you're free to work with whimsy, using themed toys, novelty items, perhaps a book of career-related cartoons or a coffee mug with a clever slogan.

- **Is it a gift they'll really use?** Then include some actual tools of the trade: pencils and paper for an illustrator, a toolbox for a handyman, stylish desk supplies for someone who's in an office all day.

- **Is it meant for one person or many?** If you're sending a professional basket to a group of people—the teachers at your child's school, the support staff in a client's or vendor's office—fill it with foods they can all share or with multiples of a single fun item, such as sticky note pads with jokes that fit your theme.

## $ Dollar Saver Tip

You can set a loved one up to start a new job in style—without setting yourself back a bundle. Shop at an office-supply store for simple desk supplies that make a visual impact (such as a bouquet of #2 pencils or colorful pens); for a personal touch, frame a favorite photo or give an item that belonged to you, such as a keepsake paperweight.

## Basket Idea

Pack an old-fashioned doctor's bag with an overworked med student's survival kit: travel-size toiletries for long nights on call, snacks for energy, an eye mask for those rare rests, and an issue of (or subscription to) a journal in their specialty.

## Helpful Hint

If your basket contains edibles, make sure to select foods that can be prepared and eaten in an office setting (shelf-stable, no cooking, minimal utensils) and that everyone in the office can enjoy.

**Above:** For an office that's delightfully feminine but still highly functional, this rose-print desk set wrapped in pretty netting is just the thing. Give it to help her get settled in a new situation, congratulate her on a promotion, or thank her for help she's given you.

**Previous Page:** Giving a basket full of money may not sound like a good way to *save* money—but it works if you use the right kind! To make a fun gift for a broker or banker (without breaking the bank), fill a glass jar or a toy safe with play $100 bills, real pennies and nickels, or chocolate coins.

**Above:** Beneath the pretty wrap at left she'll find a beautiful desk set of rose-printed paper and intricate gold-toned metalwork. A correspondence rack, a card holder, a clipboard, a paperweight, a pen in its holder—all she needs to get down to business in style.

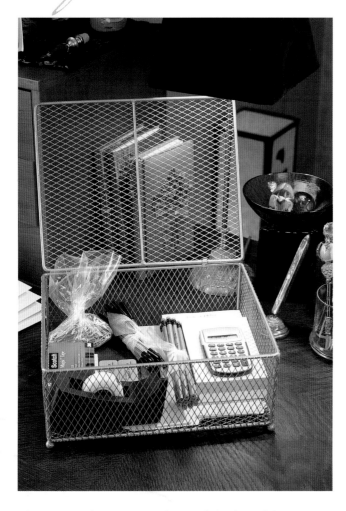

**Above:** First day at a new job (or a *first* job)? It'll be a breeze once you provide the desktop essentials—from paper clips to file folders—in a sleek wire basket set off by a few touches of mood-lightening color among the serious supplies. Later, the basket can store papers or other desk supplies.

**Above:** Help a financier get down to business with polished desk supplies (including a stapler, a tape dispenser, a letter box, and a good pen). Add an issue of an industry magazine (or a subscription, if you like). Here, it's all filed in a businesslike box with filler made of a shredded *New York Times*.

# Get Well Baskets

When someone close to you is suffering—whether with a serious illness or the small torments of the common cold—a carefully crafted gift basket is a wonderful way to show you care. Depending on the circumstances, you can fill a basket with comfort foods, pastimes to speed recovery, or flowers to brighten the day.

## Pointers for patients

More than any other type of basket, get-well gifts must be tailored to the recipient's needs:

- **Foods.** If the thought of sweets won't sit well, don't send candy or cookies. Don't include *any* food in a basket for someone who's been ill with digestive problems or had surgery that would make eating difficult.

- **Scents.** For someone who's sensitive to odors (as chemotherapy patients may be), don't send perfumed toiletries or heavily fragrant flowers such as lilies.

- **Mobility.** Someone who's housebound but basically healthy (for example, laid up with a broken leg) will appreciate help in passing the time. Choose whatever suits his or her interests: a good book, crossword puzzles or games, materials for a crafts project, a movie or a CD. For a child, include stickers or markers to decorate a cast.

### Dollar Saver Tip
Cost-conscious ways to create cheer: clip some blooms from your own garden for a personal posey, pass along a book you couldn't put down, or make a "gift certificate" for a service you'll provide while the patient's recovering (cleaning the house, cooking a meal, feeding the cats).

### Basket Idea
Pack a survival kit for a hospital stay: skin lotion and lip balm to keep her hydrated; a cozy robe or soft pair of pajamas to help him rest comfortably; family photos, a favorite object, or a stuffed toy to set on the bedside table.

### Helpful Hint
Don't assume that any illness is too minor, or too grave, for a get-well basket to be welcome. A friend bothered by a simple sore throat will enjoy a few tea bags wrapped up with a honey bear; someone fighting sickness you *can't* soothe will be touched by any gift that shows she's in your thoughts.

**Above:** Serve up chicken soup for a sick friend's soul! Here, a generous bowl holds gourmet soup mix—convenient and delicious—plus appropriate accompaniments. (Note: Soup is a soothing food to tempt a recuperating appetite, but before you send it, make sure the recipient is able to eat.)

**Previous Page:** Soothing and restorative at the same time, tea is a perfect way to help those who've been under the weather relax and regain their strength. Include whatever teatime treats are suitable for the situation, plus gifts they'll enjoy long after they're healed.

**Opposite:** Build a bouquet in a box! If you're hand-delivering this elegant gift to a patient who can enjoy fresh flowers, use moistened floral foam in a plastic-lined container to hold rows of beautiful blooms. For longer shelf life, or for someone sensitive to scents, use botanicals of silk or papier-mâché.

For someone in your life who defies categorization, set your imagination free to create a gift basket as indefinably extraordinary as he or she is! There are no rules, and this kind of basket is limited only by what you can dream up, so give yourself permission to really dream big.

## Think way outside the box

You can find inspiration for a unique gift basket in any number of places—including where you least expect it—so keep an open mind. Some possible starting points:

- **Containers.** A bowling bag, a baby carriage, a steamer trunk you spotted while traveling, a fringed silk lampshade in an antique shop—any of these could spark an idea for a unique basket.

- **Themes.** Challenge yourself to stick to one theme (cats, the Caribbean, the color orange) from container to contents to fill. It'll be fun for both you and the recipient!

- **Interests.** In this case, it's fine to combine (and you can use your sense of humor, too). Does he like old movies *and* fine wines? Send him *The Grapes of Wrath* on DVD with a good vintage to sip while he watches. Or, for a doll collector who loves to sport stylish bonnets, fill a hatbox with doll-sized hats.

### Dollar Saver Tip

To create a cost-conscious container, decoupage a plain wastebasket, using images in keeping with your theme, then fill it with budget-friendly items. (For a travel buff, decorate the container with maps and fill it with antique postcards, bought at a thrift shop or second-hand bookstore.)

### Basket Idea

Give new meaning to a "market basket" with the theme of stocks and bonds. Fill a money-patterned wastebasket with mock ticker tape (easy to make by cutting up newspaper or green-and-white printer paper). Add a stuffed bull and bear, and an issue of the *Wall Street Journal*.

### Helpful Hint

If you've dreamed up a gift basket that will be a challenge to transport (for example, a wheelbarrow full of soil and a ready-to-plant rosebush), consider setting it up on site in the recipient's home or office as a surprise.

# *Unique Baskets* continued

**Above:** An Oriental trunk sets the stage for a gift experience that's like stepping into another world—perfect for someone who dreams of visiting the Far East (or who simply appreciates beautiful things). If you set up such a display ahead of time, you can plug in the lights for a really enticing effect.

**Previous Page:** All the items in this unique presentation are birds of a feather—objects of beauty and usefulness that the recipient can use to make feath-ered friends feel welcome in his or her yard. With a weighty birdbath as a base, this basket would be easier to set up on site than to deliver or ship.

**Opposite:** An antique toy chest (carefully cleaned) sets this gift apart from run-of-the-mill children's presents. Fill it with classic and contemporary play-things; if you like, include one of your own family heirlooms to make the gift even more personal.

# Basket Business

*A*re you creating gift baskets so memorable that family and friends ask when you're going to quit your day job? Do you thank them, then think no more of it?

Maybe you *should* think more.

The gift-basket business is a $1.5 billion industry—a fast-growing field of opportunity to combine profit with personal expression. To succeed, you need almost no special equipment or training. All you really need is creativity, an entrepreneurial spirit, and a little advice to get you started.

## Planning your business

In this section, we'll help you decide whether a gift-basket business is right for you. We'll guide you through the choices and challenges you'll face—from finding your market to strategizing long-term growth—because we've faced them, too.

## Running your business

What should you charge for a fruit basket? How do you track inventory? We'll help you figure out the nuts and bolts with checklists and worksheets for developing your plan of action. And we'll guide you to find any further resources you may need.

## Thinking It Through

Ask yourself these questions, then read on for ways to refine your answers.

- Why do I want to start a gift-basket business?

- What experience do I have in business? with gift baskets?

- What are my goals for my gift-basket business—financial, professional, personal?

- How will I finance my business? What will it cost?

- Where will I house my business? How much space will I need?

- Will I have any employees?

- What will I call my business?

- How will I market my baskets to my audience?

- What kinds of baskets will I sell?

- Will I sell ready-made, or customized baskets, or a mix of the two?

- How much will I sell the baskets for?

- Where and how will I buy my inventory?

- How much inventory will I carry at one time?

- How will I deliver the baskets?

- How do these answers evolve as I look two, three, or five years ahead?

### ! Helpful Hint

These guidelines are geared primarily to a full-time gift-basket business in a store-front retail space; but if you're planning to work part-time from your home, the same principles apply. Just make a few adjustments as you read. (Example: A home-based business has no rent expenditures, but could qualify for a tax deduction.)

**Left:** Welcome customers to your store and subtly suggest opportunities for gift baskets by etching a variety of occasions on the door.

**Opposite:** Display a variety of completed baskets to help customers generate gift ideas. The containers, gift items, wrap, and ribbons may inspire an idea or two as well. Keep the display fresh by changing (or selling) the baskets on a regular basis.

## First things first

Any successful venture starts with solid research—so before you launch your gift-basket business, there are a few things you'll need to know.

### Know yourself

- Why do you want to start a basket business? Do you want the chance to use your creative skills, tap into a profitable industry, or work for your own success, not an employer's?

- What are your credentials? Have you worked with computers, held management or customer-service positions, taken classes in marketing or accounting?

- How suited are you to the life of a basket entrepreneur? Do you have what it takes to be your own boss? To test your aptitude, take our unscientific (but still revealing) quiz "Are You an Entrepreneur?"

## Are You an Entrepreneur?

Answer each question on a scale from 1 (not at all) to 5 (very much).

- Do you put goals in writing?
- Are you good at motivating people?
- Do you learn from mistakes?
- Are you organized to a fault?
- Do you get along with all kinds of people?
- Can you make quick decisions?
- Do you finish what you start?
- Is your intuition often right?
- Do you often see problems as challenges?
- Can you live with things not being perfect?
- Do you love learning about new things and ideas?
- Do you recover easily from setbacks?
- Can you maintain the motivation to work alone?
- Do people consider you to be stubborn?
- Is it easy for you to put yourself in someone else's shoes?

Now total your score. If you scored between:

**51–75:** You've got what it takes to strike out on your own.

**26–50:** You've got potential. Consider working with a partner with complementary strengths.

**15–25:** Self-employment may be more stress than success.

**Left:** Take time for an honest look at your own strengths and weaknesses. Understanding these things is key to making your business a success. That knowledge will allow you to maximize your strong points and take steps to compensate in areas you may not feel comfortable with.

### Know your market

Who will buy your baskets? Individuals or businesses? Is there a convention center, hospital, college, or other institution near you to create a core of customers? Perhaps there are niche markets you can tap, such as real estate agencies needing thank-you or welcome baskets for clients. For more details on targeting your market, see "Your marketing plan," page 119.

### Know your competition

Who else is selling baskets in your market? Your competition may include florists, grocery stores, even toy stores. Check the phone book for potential competitors; get a brochure from each company or visit its Web site. Then choose the two or three companies that impress you most and order a few of their gift baskets to get a closer look.

### Know your plan

To get your business off the ground, write up a business plan. You won't be presenting it to potential investors or lenders, at least not now; this plan is for *you*, to clarify your ideas, guide your decisions, and outline the actions you'll need to take.

Your business plan should include an action timetable with projected dates for completing each step. At the end of this section, you will find a checklist to get you started, incorporating all the elements we've discussed. To develop your plan further, you can find detailed guidelines in a number of books, magazines, and Web sites geared to small business in general and the gift-basket industry in particular.

**Left:** An enjoyable way to research the competition is to go shopping. Visit local stores that sell gift baskets. Note organization, pricing, display, variety, and types of gift items offered.

## Creating your company

Decide how to structure your business, legally and physically. Will you work alone or with a partner or employees? Buy a business or start a new one? Rent a retail space or set up shop in your garage?

### Starting from scratch

- **Pros:** The business is all yours. You make the rules, set your schedule, and reap the rewards.

- **Cons:** You assume all the risk (and invest more than an existing company requires). There are no operational or accounting procedures in place, and no customer base.

### Buying a business

- **Pros:** Procedures, suppliers, and client base are already in place. Projections are easier, because you have a history to work from.

- **Cons:** An existing company may have existing *debt* or other problems you'll inherit.

### Options for Organizing

- A **sole proprietorship**, in which one person owns all the company's assets and assumes all the liability.

- A **partnership**, which has two or more owners. This arrangement requires a legal agreement that sets forth who will contribute how much capital, how decisions will be made, disputes resolved, how profits will be shared, and how the partnership can be dissolved.

- A **corporation**, the most common form of business organization. A corporation's total worth is divided into shares of stock, each representing a unit of ownership, and shareholders participate in profits without any personal liability.

- A **limited liability company (LLC)** or **Subchapter S corporation** (named for a section of the Internal Revenue Code). These are hybrid forms of small-business organization and are taxed like partnerships but shield shareholders from personal liability, as corporations do.

A lawyer can help you set up your business according to the best option for you.

### Working from home

- **Pros:** You'll have lower overhead, some tax benefits, and more flexibility in your schedule. Being home can be an advantage in itself (if, for example, you're caring for children).

- **Cons:** You may feel isolated or lack privacy. You'll need discipline to keep your work life and your personal life separate. No storefront will mean more advertising is required to promote your baskets.

## Storefront

If you decide to rent a separate space, consider a short lease with an option to renew. You'll pay slightly higher rent, but you will be able to test the location's suitability with less risk.

### Storefront Shopping List

- Is the building in a good area with high traffic flow?

- Is there room for a highly visible sign?

- Is there adequate storage?

- Is there enough parking for customers?

- Is there room for expansion?

- Who is responsible for remodeling the space?

- Who is responsible for building upkeep?

- Will you pay other bills on top of rent (electricity, heat, maintenance)?

- Are there any zoning issues?

## Shared space

A noncompeting business might display your baskets and brochures, then get a commission for orders they take or baskets they sell. Or you might use part of another business's space for your own work. Be sure to clarify how much space your business will have, how much you'll pay in rent and expenses, and who's responsible for what.

**Below:** The name, logo, and colors you choose will become your printed identity. It is used in a variety of printed materials such as letterhead, business cards, gift enclosures, and advertising.

## Choosing a name

Your company name is a very personal statement of identity and image. Choose a short, descriptive name that is easy to spell, pronounce, and remember (and not too close to a competitor's). Aim for a name that will work well with a logo.

## Money matters

### Startup costs

You can't put a price on success, but you *can* calculate what it will cost to get your business started. Work out monthly expenses, plus any one-time costs (see The Cost of Doing Business for a guide). Then plan on setting aside funds to subsidize the business for up to three years, to cover you until you turn a profit (and see you through periods of slow basket sales).

### Resources

More than three-fourths of small business owners tap their own savings to launch their companies. You may take out a bank loan or a mortgage, borrow against a life-insurance policy, or take on a partner. But don't borrow from friends or family except as a last resort (and be sure to put it in writing).

---

**The Cost of Doing Business**

- Rent

- Salaries (your own and any employees')

- Legal and professional fees

- Insurance

- Office supplies and equipment

- Store displays and equipment

- Basket supplies and inventory (initial outlay, special orders, busy times of year)

- Trade-show attendance

- Magazine subscriptions

- Advertising

---

**$ Dollar Saver Tip**

A good rule of thumb for financing your business: never borrow more than you can afford to lose.

---

### Account-ability

Hire an accountant to set up bookkeeping procedures, file your taxes, and prevent problems down the road. Don't blindly trust *anyone* with your finances; be sure you understand the procedures so you can review reports yourself.

## Legal matters

### Hire a lawyer

Even if your business is starting small, a good lawyer's services are a smart investment. He or she will trademark your name, help you incorporate, help you protect yourself against liability, and stay abreast of small-business law so you don't have to.

### Follow the rules

You will need to register your business name with local and state officials; obtain various licenses, including a resale license, a state sales and use tax permit, and a federal tax identification number; and meet other requirements, from zoning laws to health regulations. Your lawyer's help will make these matters simple.

### Get covered

What happens if someone slips on the way into your store? If your inventory is damaged by a flood? Proper insurance can protect you against loss, theft, and liability. If you work at home, check your homeowner's or renter's policy to see if it covers business activities.

## Your marketing plan

Don't hide your baskets under a bushel! To get your business the attention it deserves, you'll need a marketing plan that addresses the following points.

### Target markets

Brainstorm potential clients and list them by categories: real-estate agencies, mortgage companies, business groups you belong to (include your Chamber of Commerce), hotel concierges and PR managers, doctors who perform elective surgery (they often give flowers or gift baskets to patients), executives of local corporations (contact their assistants first).

---

**Helpful Hint**

Who buys baskets? Nationwide research shows that the most frequent gift basket buyers are corporate accounts and women ages 26–60.

---

### Partnering

See if you can partner with area businesses to fill *and* sell your baskets. For example, you might include scented candles from a local shop, then display your baskets in the shop. Work out fees beforehand.

### Advertising and promotions

Seize every chance to advertise for free! Send news releases to the local paper, write an article for a community newsletter, donate baskets to charity events as prizes, or chair an event yourself to attract new customers to your area.

When paying for advertising, ask yourself:

- What is the target market?

- What message do you want to send?

- What product do you want to emphasize?

- What return do you expect?

- What is your advertising budget per week? month? year?

Then consider how best to reach the audience and convey the message. You can get the word out with print advertising in newspapers or the phone book, by printed flyers or direct mail, on a Web site, and, of course, by word of mouth.

### The personal touch

Keep your client base strong by keeping in touch. If you see an article in the paper about a local businessperson, send him or her a note

---

**Planning for Profits**

The slowest sales months of the year are January, March, July, August, September, and October. Most gift baskets are sold around Valentine's Day, Mothers' Day, Christmas, and large local corporate events. Most gift-basket companies count on the weeks between November 15 and December 20 for 50%–75% of their business.

---

of congratulations with your business card. Send clients birthday cards, holiday cards, or "reminder" cards (useful to jog a husband's memory about an anniversary or Valentine's Day). They'll remember to send the gifts—and they'll remember *you*.

## Setting up shop

### Display

Decorate your window to entice customers in, then set up your showroom with gifts, wrappings, and finished baskets to showcase the quality and imagination in every step. Make sure you have room for customers to browse, plus a counter area with a cash register, a credit-card station, and supplies.

### Work area

For efficient basket building, you'll need a long, flat work surface, plus room to keep baskets, gifts, and assembly materials close at hand. Have a place to store completed baskets until they are delivered or shipped.

### Office

Outfit your office with a desk, a computer and printer, a file cabinet, a copy machine, and a fax machine. Organize your supplies: letterhead, business cards, brochures, receipts. Then organize *yourself* with a good planner, whether it's a PDA, a computer program, or a book with several sections. Finally, set up systems (paper or electronic) to index client and vendor names, track inventory, and keep the books.

### Shipping and receiving

Set aside space for materials on their way in and baskets on their way out. You'll need storage for supplies; file space for orders in progress and

completed orders; a flat surface to fill out forms; room to pack; and a holding area for baskets waiting to be shipped. (For more on shipping, see "Delivering the goods," page 124.)

## Perfecting your product

Will you focus on fruit baskets? baby baskets? corporate gifts? Use the categories you plan to offer as a guide for the supplies and gift inventory you'll need:

- Containers in a range of sizes and styles

- Food and gift items that can be used to build a number of different baskets. In each category (crackers, bath products), buy one budget line and one for high-end baskets

- Filler for base support and for visible support

- Decorative wrapping and a shrink-wrap machine

---

### Keep Orders in Order

Some things to keep in mind when you place an order with a vendor:

- What's the shelf life of the merchandise?

- How quickly will it arrive?

- Will items on backorder be shipped automatically?

- Will the vendor supply samples? Free or for a fee?

- Must items be ordered by the full case or can they be mixed?

- Is there a minimum dollar or quantity amount for orders or re-orders?

- What are the payment terms—COD, credit card, "net 30"?

- What's the return policy? Is there a restocking fee?

- If you are buying items at a trade show, is there a "show special"?

Once the order is placed, get a copy of it from the vendor and double-check each item. Don't be afraid to ask questions if you're unsure of anything.

---

**Opposite Left:** Simple metal shelves hold gift items for customers' shopping convenience. These shelves are used throughout the store, both on the showroom floor and in the back work areas for storage.

**Opposite Right:** Colored fill material is stored in galvanized tubs behind the front counter for easy access.

**Left:** A shipping and receiving area doesn't need to be fancy to be useful. A computer, a printer, a scale, shelves to hold supplies and a stool or chair fills the shipping bill nicely.

**Left:** Simple, adjustable wire shelving hold basket inventory above a workspace behind the showroom. Adjustable shelves are preferred because they allow you to accomodate a variety of heights and sizes as your inventory changes.

**Below:** The counter holds a roll of wrapping paper and other supplies for assembling baskets. The containers for baskets are stored below the counter for quick access. Stacks of baskets stored on upper shelves are a safety hazard. They can be deceptively heavy and cause an injury when you are trying to retrieve a basket.

**! Helpful Hint**
A counter is useful for a large order of baskets that can be made assembly-line style. Below the counter is also a good spot to store ready-made baskets until they are rotated onto the showroom floor.

- Ribbons and twine in colors that can be used for multiple basket types

- Embellishments (such as curling ribbon and small gifts) to use as inexpensive filler

- Supplements, such as foods and decorative items, to display to tempt customers looking for a stand-alone gift

## Stocking your shelves

Before you shop for inventory:

- Subscribe to trade magazines to get ideas, track trends, and identify vendors.

- Attend trade shows to gather catalogs, ask questions, and list supplies you'll need.

- Project the number of baskets you must sell each day for one year to meet overhead. Use these projections to guide your inventory and supply buying.

When you're ready to stock up, you can buy direct from manufacturers at shows, through distributors, through trade publications or catalogs, from warehouse clubs (which pass along deep discounts), or from retailers (if you need just a few items). You can also partner with artisans in your area to offer products your competition can't.

To keep tabs on your stock, consider a computerized tracking system. You'll need to account for damaged goods and returns, track shelf life of perishables, and keep an eye on supply so you won't run out of something you need.

### Dollar Saver Tip
Once a year or a season, many vendors sell leftover merchandise at closeout prices. You may find great deals on otherwise expensive items. Make sure that the items you choose have no flaws that would make them unappealing or unusable.

## Pricing your product

Plan to make baskets in low, medium, and high price ranges.

### Keystone pricing

Calculate the wholesale cost of the basket and all its contents. Include the cost of the container, filler, wrap, and ribbon. Add a charge for wrapping labor and the shipping cost you incurred for the items in the basket. Once you've calculated the total cost, double it. This 100% markup is called "keystone."

### Mixed markups

If doubling the cost of everything in the basket is prohibitive (for example, if you've used one or two very expensive items), double the cost of the less expensive contents, including wrapping and shipping costs. Then add 20% to the cost of the high-priced item(s).

### Helpful Hint
According to a nationwide survey, the average price of the best-selling gift basket is $25 to $40.

### Wrapping services

Customers may ask you to wrap baskets and gifts they provide. For you, this is a better chance for promotion than for profit. Set fees for wrapping small, medium, and large baskets based on the cost of materials and labor.

## Delivering the goods

Your baskets must arrive safe and on time; your reputation depends on it (and so do the fresh fruit and fragile glass you've packed!). Open accounts with one or two carriers you can trust. Make sure they:

- Pick up daily.

- Offer several delivery options (overnight, second-day, and third-day air; ground delivery; Saturday delivery).

- Send invoices monthly.

- Offer automated tracking.

- Provide instructions for preparing packages and filing claims.

- Offer training and support for using their system.

- Provide good customer service (because when they deliver your baskets, they're representing you).

---

**$ Dollar Saver Tip**

Shipping supplies for free! Large companies that receive goods packed in peanuts, bubble wrap, or other packing materials may save them for you to pick up weekly, if you ask. Some large stores may also save their boxes for you.

---

## Growing your business

You're off to a wonderful start—but where do you go from here? Where do you want to be in two, three, four, or five years?

To keep your business moving in a dynamic direction, make a long-range plan for years two through five, projecting changes—and their costs—in all the aspects of the business we've discussed: company structure, target market, workspace, inventory, and suppliers.

Will you need someone to share the workload? Will you be ready to seek out larger orders, higher-profile clients, more creative challenges? How can you enhance your skills and expand your network? Distill your ideas into specific steps you can

take and set target dates for completing each one.

But first, use our Countdown to Launch action plan on page 126 to gear you up for your Grand Opening—and let us wish you luck in your brand-new basket business!

---

### Reasons for Failure

- Poor business plan

- Failure to retain professional services (legal, accounting)

- Cash-flow problems due to inadequate reserves

- Poor understanding of your market

- Poor understanding of your competition

- Pricing your goods and services too low for profit or too high to be competitive

- Too-narrow customer base (don't rely on one large client)

- Failure to foresee change in your community or customers

- Trying to be everything to everybody

- Trying to do everything yourself

---

## Rules for Success

- Plan for success: create short-term and long-term business plans to spell out where you're going and how to get there.

- Accept change: learn to react and recover quickly when things don't go as planned.

- Know your customer: study how your target market shops and what they buy.

- Serve your customer: set and follow strict guidelines for customer service.

- Build a reputation: be known for quality, creativity, service, and integrity.

- Find a niche: focus on a product, a service, or a degree of quality that sets you apart.

**Right Above and Below:** An organized counter functions as a display and a work space. The cash register computer monitor is disguised so it won't detract from the displays.

## Countdown to Launch

Customize this checklist to your particular plans, then use it to stay on schedule as the big day nears!

- What will you do to improve your credentials?
  _____
  _____
  Target date _____ Completed _____

- How will you evaluate your competitors?
  _____
  Target date _____ Completed _____

- How will you raise the funds for each item in your financial plan?
  _____
  Target date _____ Completed _____

- When will you pay back borrowed funds?
  _____
  _____
  Target date _____ Completed _____

- When will you begin each phase of your marketing plan?
  _____
  _____
  Target date _____ Completed _____

- What basket supplies will you buy?
  _____
  _____
  Target date _____ Completed _____

- What office supplies and equipment will you buy?
  _____
  Target date _____ Completed _____

- When will you set up your office?
  _____
  Target date _____ Completed _____

- What delivery or courier service will you contract with?
  _____
  _____
  Target date _____ Completed _____

- When will you buy and organize shipping supplies?
  _____
  Target date _____ Completed _____

- When will you obtain each license or certificate needed?
  _____
  Target date _____ Completed _____

- When will you open for business? _____
  _____

# Author's Note

Nothing of what I accomplish every day would be possible without the incredible help and support of my amazing team. To all of my employees who make coming to work every day a joy—thank you. Most of all to Ashly, the stores' manager, you are a godsend and I value your creativity, insight, and willingness to step up to the plate more than you will ever know. Thank you for all of your hard work on this book.

To my mom, my business partner and best friend, and the one responsible for my creative side, thank you for encouraging me to follow my dreams and helping me make them all come true.

To my dad, the one responsible for my "Type A" side, you are my role model and motivation to better myself. Thank you for helping me attain any goal I have ever set.

And to my wonderful husband, with whom my best moments have been spent and all of my best adventures are about to begin. Thank you for making me smile every day.

# Metric Equivalency Charts

## inches to millimeters and centimeters

| inches | mm | cm | inches | cm | inches | cm |
|---|---|---|---|---|---|---|
| ⅛ | 3 | 0.3 | 9 | 22.9 | 30 | 76.2 |
| ¼ | 6 | 0.6 | 10 | 25.4 | 31 | 78.7 |
| ½ | 13 | 1.3 | 12 | 30.5 | 33 | 83.8 |
| ⅝ | 16 | 1.6 | 13 | 33.0 | 34 | 86.4 |
| ¾ | 19 | 1.9 | 14 | 35.6 | 35 | 88.9 |
| ⅞ | 22 | 2.2 | 15 | 38.1 | 36 | 91.4 |
| 1 | 25 | 2.5 | 16 | 40.6 | 37 | 94.0 |
| 1¼ | 32 | 3.2 | 17 | 43.2 | 38 | 96.5 |
| 1½ | 38 | 3.8 | 18 | 45.7 | 39 | 99.1 |
| 1¾ | 44 | 4.4 | 19 | 48.3 | 40 | 101.6 |
| 2 | 51 | 5.1 | 20 | 50.8 | 41 | 104.1 |
| 2½ | 64 | 6.4 | 21 | 53.3 | 42 | 106.7 |
| 3 | 76 | 7.6 | 22 | 55.9 | 43 | 109.2 |
| 3½ | 89 | 8.9 | 23 | 58.4 | 44 | 111.8 |
| 4 | 102 | 10.2 | 24 | 61.0 | 45 | 114.3 |
| 4½ | 114 | 11.4 | 25 | 63.5 | 46 | 116.8 |
| 5 | 127 | 12.7 | 26 | 66.0 | 47 | 119.4 |
| 6 | 152 | 15.2 | 27 | 68.6 | 48 | 121.9 |
| 7 | 178 | 17.8 | 28 | 71.1 | 49 | 124.5 |
| 8 | 203 | 20.3 | 29 | 73.7 | 50 | 127.0 |

## yards to meters

| yards | meters | yards | meters | yards | meters | yards | meters | yards | meters |
|---|---|---|---|---|---|---|---|---|---|
| ⅛ | 0.11 | 2⅛ | 1.94 | 4⅛ | 3.77 | 6⅛ | 5.60 | 8⅛ | 7.43 |
| ¼ | 0.23 | 2¼ | 2.06 | 4¼ | 3.89 | 6¼ | 5.72 | 8¼ | 7.54 |
| ⅜ | 0.34 | 2⅜ | 2.17 | 4⅜ | 4.00 | 6⅜ | 5.83 | 8⅜ | 7.66 |
| ½ | 0.46 | 2½ | 2.29 | 4½ | 4.11 | 6½ | 5.94 | 8½ | 7.77 |
| ⅝ | 0.57 | 2⅝ | 2.40 | 4⅝ | 4.23 | 6⅝ | 6.06 | 8⅝ | 7.89 |
| ¾ | 0.69 | 2¾ | 2.51 | 4¾ | 4.34 | 6¾ | 6.17 | 8¾ | 8.00 |
| ⅞ | 0.80 | 2⅞ | 2.63 | 4⅞ | 4.46 | 6⅞ | 6.29 | 8⅞ | 8.12 |
| 1 | 0.91 | 3 | 2.74 | 5 | 4.57 | 7 | 6.40 | 9 | 8.23 |
| 1⅛ | 1.03 | 3⅛ | 2.86 | 5⅛ | 4.69 | 7⅛ | 6.52 | 9⅛ | 8.34 |
| 1¼ | 1.14 | 3¼ | 2.97 | 5¼ | 4.80 | 7¼ | 6.63 | 9¼ | 8.46 |
| 1⅜ | 1.26 | 3⅜ | 3.09 | 5⅜ | 4.91 | 7⅜ | 6.74 | 9⅜ | 8.57 |
| 1½ | 1.37 | 3½ | 3.20 | 5½ | 5.03 | 7½ | 6.86 | 9½ | 8.69 |
| 1⅝ | 1.49 | 3⅝ | 3.31 | 5⅝ | 5.14 | 7⅝ | 6.97 | 9⅝ | 8.80 |
| 1¾ | 1.60 | 3¾ | 3.43 | 5¾ | 5.26 | 7¾ | 7.09 | 9¾ | 8.92 |
| 1⅞ | 1.71 | 3⅞ | 3.54 | 5⅞ | 5.37 | 7⅞ | 7.20 | 9⅞ | 9.03 |
| 2 | 1.83 | 4 | 3.66 | 6 | 5.49 | 8 | 7.32 | 10 | 9.14 |

# Index

## A

A basket for all reasons . . . . . . . . . . . 72
A gallery of gifts . . . . . . . . . . . . . . . . 29
A man, a plan, a basket . . . . . . . . . . 46
Account-ability . . . . . . . . . . . . . . . . 118
Advertising and promotions . . . . . . . 119
All Occasion Baskets . . . . . . . . . 72–97
Are You an Entrepreneur? . . . . . . . 114
Author's Note . . . . . . . . . . . . . . . . . 127

## B

Baby and Child Baskets . . . . . . . . 52–65
Basket Basics . . . . . . . . . . . . . 5, 8–27
Basket Brainstorming . . . . . . . . . . . . 10
Basket Business . . . . . . . . . 5, 110–126
Basket Gallery . . . . . . . . . 5, 28–109
Basket Worksheet . . . . . . . . . . . . . . 27
Baskets for whomever, whenever, whyever
. . . . . . . . . . . . . . . . . . . . . . . . . . . . 5
Bountiful Basket, 50 . . . . . . . . . . . . 11
Building your basket . . . . . . . . . . . . . 12
Buying a business . . . . . . . . . . . . . . 116

## C

Candy roses . . . . . . . . . . . . . . . . . . 18
Cautions to consider . . . . . . . . . . . . 10
Choose a container . . . . . . . . . . . . . 13
Choosing a name . . . . . . . . . . . . . . 117
Considering the Competition . . . . . 115
Container . . . . . . . . . . . . . . . . . . . . 12
corporation . . . . . . . . . . . . . . . . . . 116
Countdown to Launch . . . . . . . . . . 126
Creating your company . . . . . . . . . 116

## D

Delivering the goods . . . . . . . . . . . 124
Display . . . . . . . . . . . . . . . . . . . . . 120

## F

Family Baskets . . . . . . . . . . . . . . 66–71
Feminine Baskets . . . . . . . . . . . . 40–45
Filler . . . . . . . . . . . . . . . . . . . . . . . 12
First things first . . . . . . . . . . . . . . . 114
Floral picks . . . . . . . . . . . . . . . . . . 17
Florist's bow . . . . . . . . . . . . . . . . . 26
Follow the rules . . . . . . . . . . . . . . 118
Food for thought . . . . . . . . . . . . . . 30

## G

Get covered . . . . . . . . . . . . . . . . . 119
Get Well Baskets . . . . . . . . . 102–105
Gift items . . . . . . . . . . . . . . . . . . . 12
glue dots . . . . . . . . . . . . . . . . 13, 19

Gourmet Baskets . . . . . . . . . . . 30–35
Growing your business . . . . . . . . . 124

## H

Handle with care . . . . . . . . . . . . . . 52
Hands-on how-to's . . . . . . . . . . . . . 13
Hire a lawyer . . . . . . . . . . . . . . . . 118
How to use this book . . . . . . . . . . . . 5

## I

Introduction . . . . . . . . . . . . . . . . . . 5

## K

Keep Orders in Order . . . . . . . . . . 121
Keystone pricing . . . . . . . . . . . . . . 123
Know your competition . . . . . . . . . 115
Know your market . . . . . . . . . . . . . 115
Know your plan . . . . . . . . . . . . . . . 115
Know yourself . . . . . . . . . . . . . . . . 114

## L

Legal matters . . . . . . . . . . . . . . . . 118
limited liability company . . . . . . . . 116
LLC . . . . . . . . . . . . . . . . . . . . . . . 116

## M

Make a basket look full . . . . . . . . . . 16
Make a floral foam base . . . . . . . . . 14
Make a fruit basket foam base . . . . . 14
Make special interests special . . . . . . 40
Masculine Baskets . . . . . . . . . . . 46–51
Metric Equivalency Charts . . . . . . . 127
Mixed markups . . . . . . . . . . . . . . . 123
Money matters . . . . . . . . . . . . . . . 118

## O

Office . . . . . . . . . . . . . . . . . . . . . . 120
Options for Organizing . . . . . . . . . 116

## P

Pack breakable items . . . . . . . . . . . 16
Pack items in filler . . . . . . . . . . . . . 15
Partnering . . . . . . . . . . . . . . . . . . 119
partnership . . . . . . . . . . . . . . . . . 116
Perfecting your product . . . . . . . . . 121
Planning for Profits . . . . . . . . . . . . 119
Planning your basket . . . . . . . . . . . 10
Planning your business . . . . . . . . . 111
Pointers for patients . . . . . . . . . . . 102
Pricing your product . . . . . . . . . . . 123
Professional Baskets . . . . . . . . . 98–101

## Q

Questions to ask . . . . . . . . . . . . . . 66

## R

Reasons for Failure . . . . . . . . . . . . 124
Resources . . . . . . . . . . . . . . . . . . . 118
Ribbon sprays . . . . . . . . . . . . . . . . 17
Rules for relaxation . . . . . . . . . . . . 36
Rules for Success . . . . . . . . . . . . . 125
Running your business . . . . . . . . . . 111

## S

Setting up shop . . . . . . . . . . . . . . 120
Shared space . . . . . . . . . . . . . . . . 117
Shipping and receiving . . . . . . . . . 120
Shrink wrap . . . . . . . . . . . . . . . . . 20
sole proprietorship . . . . . . . . . . . . 116
Spa Baskets . . . . . . . . . . . . . . . 36–39
Stack items around a basket . . . . . . 19
Starting from scratch . . . . . . . . . . 116
Startup costs . . . . . . . . . . . . . . . . 118
Stocking your shelves . . . . . . . . . . 123
Storefront . . . . . . . . . . . . . . . . . . 117
Storefront Shopping List . . . . . . . . 117
Subchapter S corporation . . . . . . . 116

## T

Target markets . . . . . . . . . . . . . . . 119
The Cost of Doing Business . . . . . . 118
The personal touch . . . . . . . . . . . . 119
Think outside the gift box . . . . . . . . 9
Think way outside the box . . . . . . . 106
Thinking it Through . . . . . . . . . . . 112
Tie a ribbon and tag the gift . . . . . . 22
Tissue . . . . . . . . . . . . . . . . . . . . . 18

## U

Unique Baskets . . . . . . . . . . . 106–109
Use decorative filler . . . . . . . . . . . 17
Using a heat gun or blow-dryer . . . . 20
Using a shrink-wrap machine . . . . . 21

## W

Work area . . . . . . . . . . . . . . . . . . 120
Work is your basket! . . . . . . . . . . . 98
Working from home . . . . . . . . . . . 116
Wrap a basket in cellophane, netting,
or other wrap . . . . . . . . . . . . . . . 20
Wrapping . . . . . . . . . . . . . . . . . . . 12
Wrapping services . . . . . . . . . . . . . 123

## Y

Your marketing plan . . . . . . . . . . . 119